String Time Joggers

14 pieces for flexible ensemble

Kathy and David Blackwell

Contents

This symbol indicates the CD track numbers for each piece. The top number indicates the complete performance, and the bottom number the accompaniment alone.
A tuning note (A) is located on track 29.

Violin

Sea Suite

1. Shark attack!

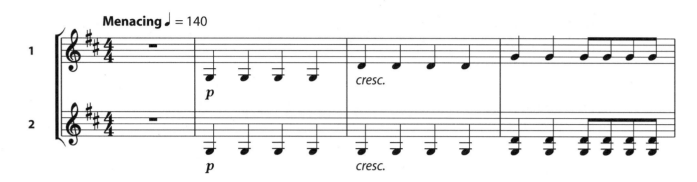

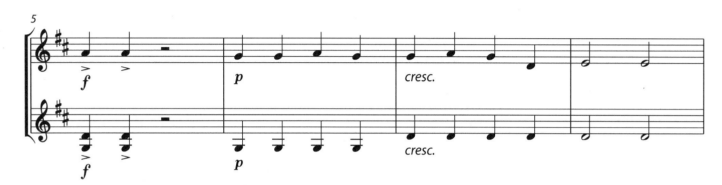

Printed in Great Britain

OXFORD UNIVERSITY PRESS, MUSIC DEPARTMENT, GREAT CLARENDON STREET, OXFORD OX2 6DP

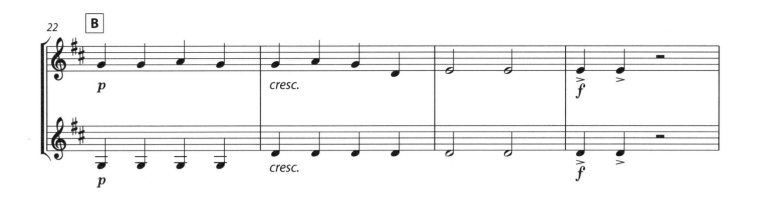

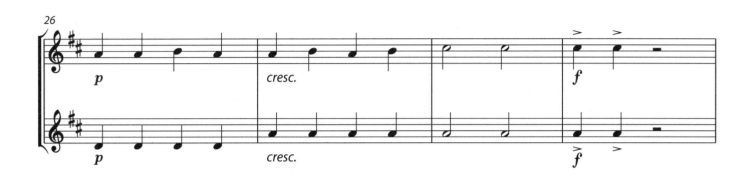

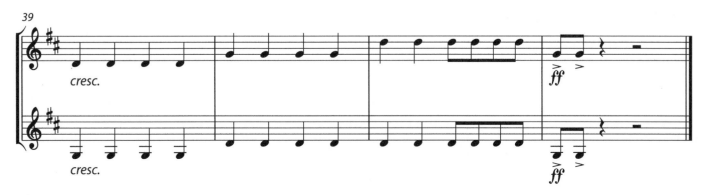

2. Barrier Reef

3. Cap'n Jack's Hornpipe

Lively ♩ = 84

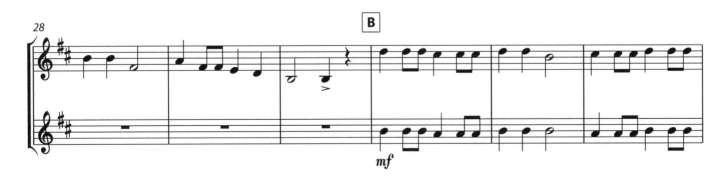

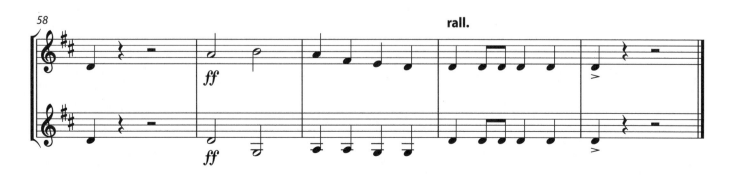

4. Simple Syncopation

Happy ♩ = 112

5. Feelin' blue

Slow and moody ♩ = 68

Fine

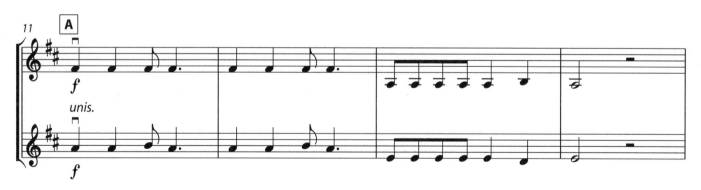

D.S. al Fine

6. Broadway or bust

Bright swing ♩ = 112

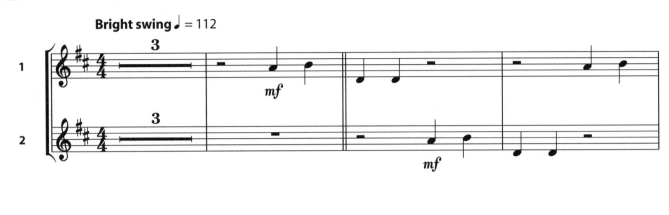

A

7. Tinga Layo

(Part 1 and Harmony)

West Indian Trad.

7. Tinga Layo

(Part 2)

West Indian Trad.

8. Jamaican lullaby

Jamaican Trad.

Gently flowing ♩ = 104

9. Kingston Calypso

(Part 2)

9. Kingston Calypso

(Part 1 and Harmony)

Sunny ♩ = 130

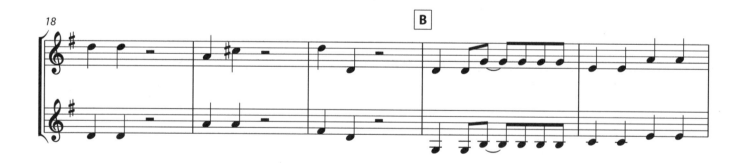

Hollywood Suite

10. Spy movie 2

Menacing ♩ = 130

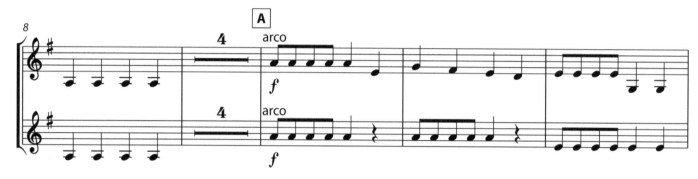

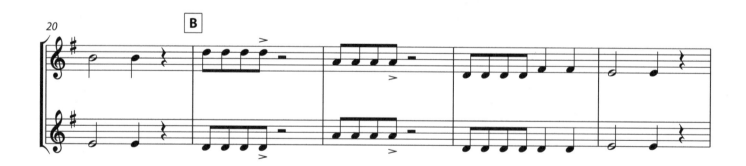

11. Sad movie

20

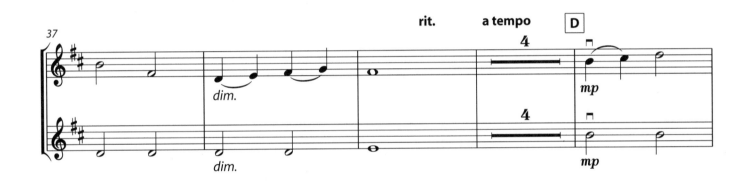

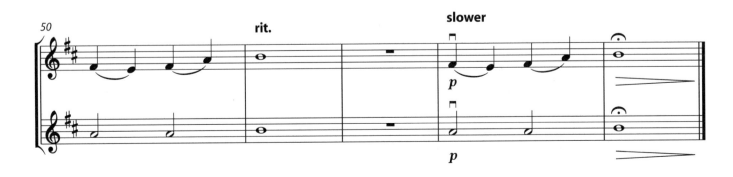

12. Action movie

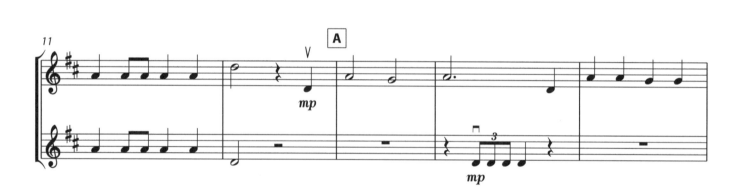

MELODY

OSTINATO

14. Banuwa

MELODY

African Trad.

OSTINATO